The BIG MAN'S LITTLE BOOK

Jesus 2000 years on

NICK HARDING

First published in 1999 by
KEVIN MAYHEW LTD
Buxhall
Stowmarket
Suffolk IP14 3BW

© 1999 Nick Harding

The right of Nick Harding to be identified
as the author of this work has been asserted
by him in accordance with the Copyright,
Designs and Patents Act 1988.

All rights reserved.

Material in this book is copyright-free provided that it is used
for the purpose for which the book is intended. The usual
copyright restrictions apply to any use for commercial purposes.

0 1 2 3 4 5 6 7 8 9

ISBN 1 84003 412 2
Catalogue Number 1500302

Cover illustration by Jonathan Stroulger
Edited by Helen Elliot
Typesetting by Kevin Whomes
Printed and bound in Great Britain

Acknowledgements

Thanks to Clare, the boys, and Rivendell

*For all children who have heard of Jesus
but want to know who he really is
and what he really did
– this one's for you!*

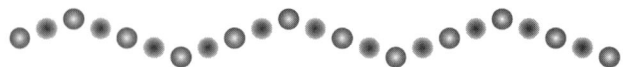

1. Who is the 'Big Man'?

We don't know what the Big Man looked like. We don't know if he was tall or small. We don't know how he spoke, what his smile was like, or even how smelly his feet were. But we do know roughly when he lived and died. We know he said amazing things, he helped hundreds of people, and he died the death of a criminal by being hung on a cross. We also know that after dying he came alive again, beating death forever!

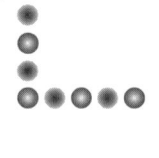

The Big Man changed history, and changed the way we record the passing of time. For the last two thousand years, two millennia, the Big

Man's birthday has been remembered by the calendar we now use. Every year from 1 to 1999 and beyond is described as AD, which means 'after the Big Man's birth'. Every year thousands of people have heard about the Big Man and have decided what he said makes sense to them. He is the Big Man because his life story is the biggest and best there has ever been.

We find out more about the Big Man from the Big Book we call the Bible. It has hundreds of stories about the Big Man in four books written by four men called Matthew, Mark, Luke and John. Use the suggestions on each page for other stories you could read from the Big Book.

This little book gives you a little look at the Big Man, and the Big Man is called Jesus.

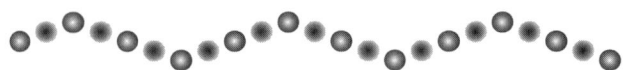

2. What's in a life?

Before you read the rest of this book (which I hope you will do!) have a quick think about yourself. Who are you, and who chose your name? Where were you born? Who came to visit you after you were born? What do you plan to do in your life? How long do you hope to live?

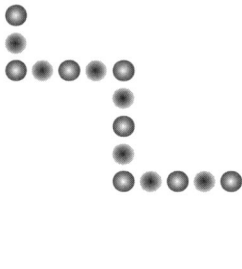

Now you know all about yourself try to imagine the life of a boy whose name was announced to his parents by an angel, and who was born in a smelly, damp and dark cattle shed. Think how weird it would be to be visited by a load of farmers from the local fields and a group of rich brain-boxes from another country who said they'd followed a star! Then get your head around the idea of the boy growing up to be a man who lived to help others, never did anything wrong, and was killed for no good reason. Add to that the fact that the dead man came alive again, and you've got an extraordinary person and an amazing story. Read on . . .

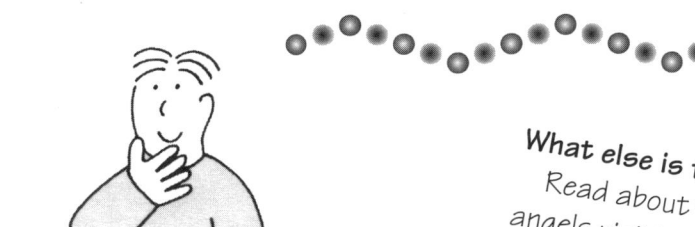

What now?
Make a list of all the things you know about the Big Man called Jesus. Then read on to find out more.

What else is there?
Read about the angels visiting Mary and Joseph:
Luke 1:26-38,
Matthew 1:20-21.

3. What's in the sky?

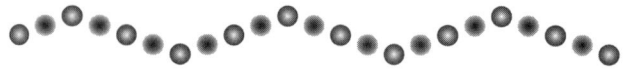

Have you ever looked up at the sky late at night? There are many hundreds of stars, some close enough to see and others way beyond our vision. It's incredible that somewhere out in space there are such bright and powerful lights.

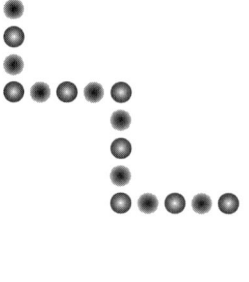

There were three very clever men who probably lived in the Continent we now call Asia. They studied maps and books, and knew that there were writings about a bright star that would lead to a new King. This sounded exciting, so the three Wise Men decided to have an adventure following the star and seeing where it led them. Each night, while it was cool, they rode as far as they could, the star always going ahead of them. Every day, while it was hot, they rested, ate, and got their strength up for the next bit of the journey. They didn't know how long the journey would last, and they weren't sure what they would find at the end of it, but they never gave up.

What now?
How do you think the stars got into space? Do you think they were made and put there by a great power, or are they the product of a load of chemicals, or what?

What else is there?
Read about the wise men and their journey: Matthew 2:1-2.
Find out where the stars may have come from: Psalm 136:1-9.

4. What's in the fields?

Have you ever stood leaning on a gate, looking at the countryside? Fields may look boring, but there's a lot in them! There may be animals, tractors and other machinery, scarecrows and seeds, worms or even cow dung!

In the fields around the small town of Bethlehem in Judaea there was plenty of activity, even late at night. Large flocks of sheep stood around grazing, while some shepherds met by a wall and talked about whatever shepherds talk about!

Suddenly, a person surrounded in light appeared and told them about a new king who had been born that night in a stable down in the town. Then, as the shepherds stared open-mouthed, the sky seemed to open up and a large choir of angels started to sing to them about peace and love being brought by the new baby. When it had all gone quiet, the shepherds decided to go and find out what it was all about. The sheep, meanwhile, stayed behind and tried to get over the shock!

What now?
Try to imagine you had been a shepherd that night. How would you have felt when you saw the angels and heard their song? What would you have done?

What else is there?
Read the full story of the shepherds and angels: Luke 2:8-15.
Find out about another angel in the Christmas story: Luke 1:26-33.

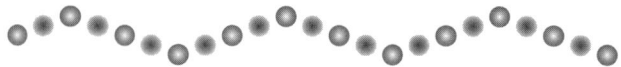

5. What's in the stable?

How would you describe a cow shed or a horse stable? I think I would say they were smelly, dirty, gross, and not places to stay for long! Certainly stables are not places to have babies in!

Mary and Joseph, a young couple from the town of Nazareth some miles away, found themselves in Bethlehem without anywhere to stay. The best they could do was to borrow a stable, dirty and smelly as it was. They got as warm and comfortable as they could before Mary

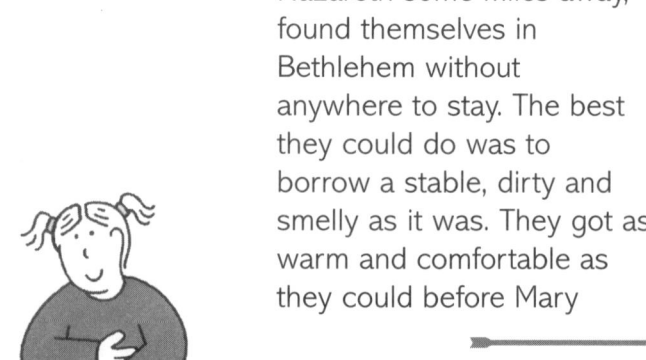

started to get pains, a sign that she was about to have a baby. Once the boy was born they wrapped him up in strips of cloth to keep him cosy and warm, and Mary rested . . . but not for long! Soon a group of shepherds arrived with a story about angels in the sky telling them to see a special baby born to be king. Later three travellers, wise men from the east, arrived with generous presents and talk of having followed a star to find the baby. Mary and Joseph both knew that their son would be special — angels had told them — but now they realised that even as a baby he was making the news!

What now?
Have a look at today's news on TV, in the papers or on the Internet (but ask permission first!). Who is making the news today? Do you think they are special people?

What else is there?
Read about when Mary and Joseph met the shepherds: Luke 2:16-20.

Discover more about the wise men at the stable: Matthew 2:9-11.

6. What's in a name?

Nearly every name has a meaning. Katherine means 'pure', Peter means 'rock', and Nick means 'winner'. Some names are common – loads of people have that name. Some are unusual. What does your name mean?

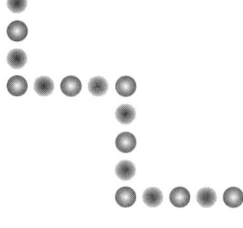

Many children were called 'Jesus' when Jesus Christ was living 2,000 years ago. So the Jesus we know about from stories of Christmas and Easter was called 'Jesus bar Joseph', which meant Jesus, son of Joseph. As he travelled around he became known as 'Jesus of Nazareth', the town where he grew up. Then people

added other names to describe him. Some called him a teacher, others called him a leader, and many had seen that he was a healer. A few called him dangerous, and a few more said he was lying about God. The ordinary people loved him, but the powerful people hated him. As Jesus was dragging along a giant cross made out of two rough planks of wood, people called him heaps of nasty and cruel names. But even as Jesus hung on the cross, nails through his wrists and ankles, a few people in the crowd watching him die knew that Jesus of Nazareth should really be called Son of God. And that's what Jesus is called now!

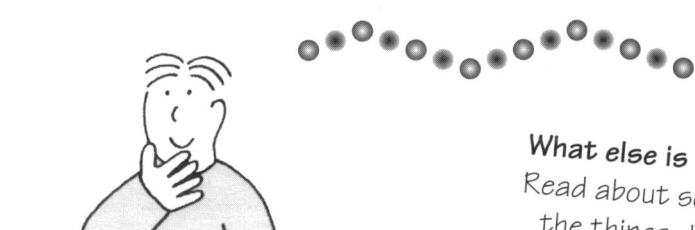

What now?
Some people use the name of Jesus as an insult, but he is worth much more than that. Do you think there's more to Jesus than just a name?

What else is there?
Read about some of the things Jesus called himself:
John 14:6.

Read what others called him:
Mark 8:27-30.

7. What's in the Father's house?

Can you remember when you were younger, and lost your mum or another adult who was with you in a crowd? You might have been really brave and looked for them, or perhaps you stood in the middle of everything and cried, shouting 'I want my mummy'! It's a really awful feeling to be lost, and it's not so nice to lose someone either.

Jesus thought that the places people went to worship – the synagogues in towns and villages and the Temple in Jerusalem – were really important places. When he was 12 he went with his parents and many thousands of others to Jerusalem for the big religious festival of Passover.

After the weekend his parents set off home, only to discover that Jesus wasn't with them. They searched everywhere they had been, and finally went to the Temple. There they found their son, sitting with the chief priests and religious teachers, who were amazed at his knowledge of God's scriptures. Jesus wasn't worried, but his parents were! I guess his mum and dad were pretty concerned that he'd gone missing, and very relieved to find him.

Throughout his life Jesus went to worship God regularly, and spoke in a number of synagogues. Not many days before he was killed he threw a load of people out of Jerusalem's Temple for using it as a market place and ripping people off.

And even now God is worshipped in many thousands of Christian churches, with his followers meeting just as Jesus did.

What now?
Jesus was special – he knew so much about God. Have a think what your special skills and abilities are, and remember – everyone is special.

What else is there?
Read about Jesus as a boy at the Temple in Jerusalem: Luke 2:41-50.

Read about Jesus in the synagogue in Nazareth: Luke 4:16-22.

8. What's in the river?

Some people really enjoy sitting on the river bank with a fishing rod, waiting for the fish to take the bait and get hooked on the end of the line. Less fortunate fishermen and women catch less attractive things such as litter, old boots or shopping trolleys! Do you like fishing? If you do, what have you found in the river?

There were some strange things happening in the River Jordan. Crowds had gathered and queues had formed to join in with what John was doing. For years John had lived wild in the desert, calling on everyone to get ready for the promised king. Now he was washing people in the river and praying for them – he was baptising them.

While John was speaking and baptising them, one after another the crowd hushed as a stranger from the village of Nazareth walked towards the river. Immediately, John stopped what he was doing and said, 'I can't baptise you! You should be the one who baptises me'. But as John and Jesus talked, John decided he had to do it – it was what God wanted. As Jesus moved towards the river bank the sky seemed to open up and what looked like a dove flew down and landed on his head. Then a loud, booming voice said, 'This is my son, and I am pleased with him.' Jesus knew that it was his Father, God, but the crowds of people didn't understand it at all.

What now?
Have you been baptised? If you have, try to find out about your baptism. If not, think about why the people decided to be baptised in the Bible stories.

What else is there?
Look at the story of Jesus being baptised: Matthew 3:13-17.

Discover another dramatic story about a baptism: Acts 8:26-40.

9. What's in the wilderness?

Close your eyes and imagine a desert or a wilderness. What do you see? Perhaps you imagine a large, hairy cactus growing up out of miles and miles of sand, or rocks and boulders scattered over a rough, dangerous land. Maybe you can picture an oasis with fountains and rich green trees, or a forbidding, dangerous mountain. One thing's for sure – a wilderness is not a nice place to be!

The Big Man, Jesus, decided to go to a wilderness area for nearly six weeks to face one of his biggest tests. He wanted to prove that he was stronger than the devil. That's why the devil came creeping along and tried to tempt Jesus to give up the work he had come to do and take up other things instead.

Jesus was getting hungry, so the devil tried to make him turn a stone into bread. Jesus could have done it, but he was strong enough to refuse.

Next the devil took Jesus to the top of a hill and showed him the whole world. 'You can be in charge of all this if you worship me instead of Father God,' he said. But Jesus stuck with what he knew was right.

Jesus knew that if he was in danger, angels would help him. The devil challenged Jesus to throw himself off the top of a cliff and get the angels to save him before he crashed onto the rocks below, but Jesus refused. 'I'm not going to test Father God,' he said, 'I trust him.' The devil was fed up with failing, and gave up. The Big Man had been tested and had won through — as he always does!

What now?
Write down a list of the things which you are tempted by. It's not good to give in to temptation, but it is often hard to do the right thing!

What else is there?
You can read about Jesus in the wilderness: Luke 4:1-13.

Look up what God says about us being tempted: Proverbs 1:10.

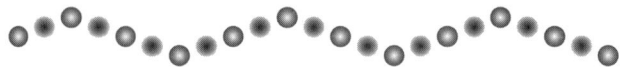

10. What's in a friend?

You have got friends, and you are a friend to others. But do you think you are a good friend? Real friends share things, have fun, stick together, share jokes they wouldn't want their parents to hear, and even get angry with each other sometimes! But the key thing about friends is that we all need them.

Jesus wanted some friends. He had been seen as the Big Man by the crowd at the River Jordan when John baptised him, and the devil had seen what a Big Man Jesus was. Now he wanted to start to change people and change the world, but he needed some people to work with him.

Jesus often walked along the beach on the edge of Lake Galilee, chatting and sharing jokes with the fishermen who were mending their nets and repairing their boats. The fishermen knew that Jesus was getting quite well known, and crowds gathered everywhere to hear what he had to say. They wanted to find out more about Jesus, so when he asked them to give up their boats for a while and help him they quickly agreed. Then a taxman left his work to go with Jesus, and so it went on. And before long Jesus' friends, the disciples, were nearly as popular as he was!

What now?
Think about how good your friends are to you, and how good a friend you are to them. Would you give up everything to help a friend?

What else is there?
Look at one of the stories of Jesus choosing his friends: Mark 1:16-20.
Read about other people who were great friends – David and Jonathan: 1 Samuel 18:1-4.

11. What's in the bandages?

There are some people who enjoy hurting others. Okay, so most of us have attacked our brothers or sisters sometime, but that's different! There are those who insult their families and friends and hurt them with hard words. Others like to hurt people by stealing things off them. Have you ever been hurt in that way?

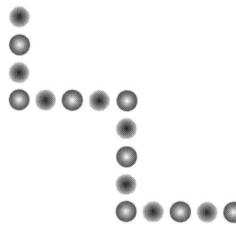

Jesus told the story of a man on a dangerous journey. He was travelling on the road from Jerusalem to Jericho with a donkey carrying his belongings. The road went through hills and rocks, and as he passed one rocky stretch he was attacked, beaten up, and left with nothing at the side of the road. His attackers thought he was dead.

After a while a priest came along the road. He saw the man lying injured, but decided to cross to the other side of the road and keep going. Later, another wealthy religious man came past and he did the same. They both ignored the pain and suffering of the beaten traveller. It was quite some time before a foreigner came past. As soon as he saw the man lying there he bandaged him up, helped him onto a donkey, and took him to a small hotel close by. There, the foreigner paid for the man to be looked after until he was well again and the bandages were no longer needed.

What now?
Are there people you know whom no one else cares about and others ignore? Could you do something to help someone who is in real need, like the boy or girl at school who no one talks to? Think about it!

What else is there?
Have a look at this story and what Jesus says about it: Luke 10:25-37.

Read how Jesus hopes we are going to care for others: Romans 15:1-2.

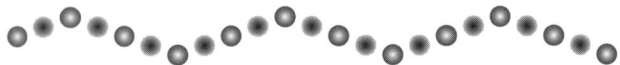

12. What's in the jars?

Have you ever had to use a well to get water to drink? Most of us are used to water coming from a tap, and plenty of it being there when we need it. And what about other drinks, such as coke or lemonade? I expect you can get hold of those easily, too.

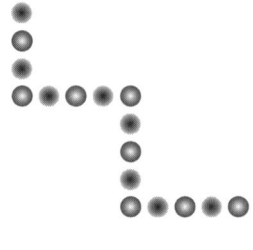

It wasn't coke or lemonade that the organisers of the party needed, it was wine! It had been a great wedding, and everyone who mattered was there. There were the leaders from the local temple, neighbours and friends, and even the man who spoke about God was

there with his mother and followers. But they were running out of food and drink fast, and everyone expected plenty of wine.

The people in charge were desperate, and Jesus saw their problem. It was so bad and embarrassing to run out of wine, and he wanted to help. He sent some servants to fill six enormous stone jars with water. With the jars of water in front of him he invited the organiser of the party to taste the water. With a look of amazement and shock the man said, 'This isn't water – somehow you've made it into wine!' Jesus smiled a little, his mother looked puzzled, and his friends were speechless!

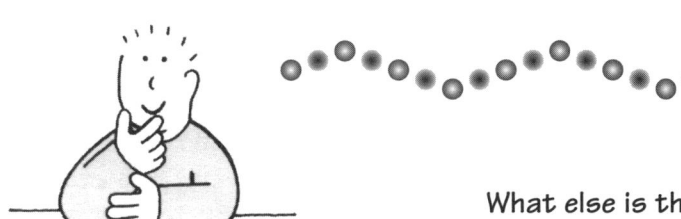

What now?
What do you think were the reasons why Jesus changed the water into wine? Was he only trying to help, or was he trying to show his friends that he was the Big Man?

What else is there?
Read the full story of Jesus at the wedding party: John 2:1-11.

13. What's in an action?

> It is great to hear someone say they care about you. I guess you're really good at telling your parents or other adults how nice they are . . . especially when you want something from them! But words alone don't mean much – actions really make a difference.

No one would have taken much notice of Jesus if he'd only used words. Like listening to a teacher, it may be interesting for a while, but then it starts to get boring! Not only did Jesus say incredible things which blew the minds of the crowds who listened to him, but he did incredible things too. Stunned fishermen watched as he walked on water, amazed villagers saw him make a blind beggar see, and snooty religious officials gasped as Jesus made people walk who had never had their feet on the ground before. These actions spoke as loud as his words, and people had to take notice. This man was something special, and news of him spread from village to village and town to town. Perhaps the most incredible thing is that news of Jesus still spreads now, 2,000 years later.

What now?
Try to imagine what it would have been like to be healed by Jesus. Do you think that people can still be healed? Read on to find out about more amazing miracles.

What else is there?
Read about Jesus healing many people: Luke 4:38-40.

Read about the first miracle Jesus did: John 2:1-11.

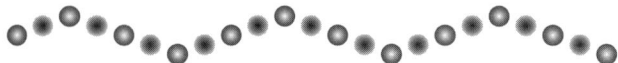

14. What's in the lunchbox?

There are lots of great things to do in the summer. There's swimming without getting too cold, and there's sunbathing and getting a little brown. There's also the chance to have picnics. What do you like in your picnic lunchbox?

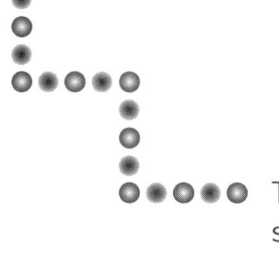

The boy decided to go and see the man who talked about God. His mum made sure he had a good lunch, and told him when to come home. She was sure he would be safe with the others from her village who were all heading up the steep hillside to hear what the Big Man, Jesus, had to say. There had been rumours that he had touched people who had got better, and 5,000 people were gathered around Jesus and his friends.

Soon the disciples realised there was a problem – they had no food to give the crowd, nor money to buy enough food. But the boy made a suggestion: 'My mum gave me these five little loaves of bread and two fish – you could share these.' Jesus took the lunchbox, prayed, and then his disciples shared it with a few people, then with ten people, then with a hundred, then with a thousand, and then five thousand . . . and still there was food left over! The people knew then that Jesus could do amazing things, and the boy who had shared his lunch knew that Jesus was really powerful.

What now?
The miracle wouldn't have happened if the boy had not been willing to share his lunchbox with Jesus. What are you willing to share?

What else is there?
Have a look at the full story of Jesus feeding 5,000: John 6:1-14.

See what Jesus says about relying on bread alone for life: Matthew 4:4.

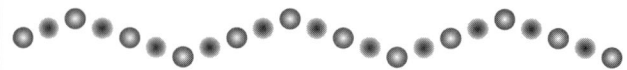

15. What's in happiness?

Are you feeling happy today? How do you know? We all have moods and the way we feel often changes from day to day. But happiness isn't just about how we feel or how big our smile is! We've also got to think about how calm, contented and happy we are inside.

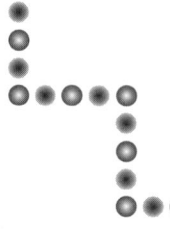

Jesus was being followed by a huge crowd of eager people all keen to hear what he'd got to say – the Big Man was becoming a Big Attraction! He led his disciples up a hill where they all sat down while

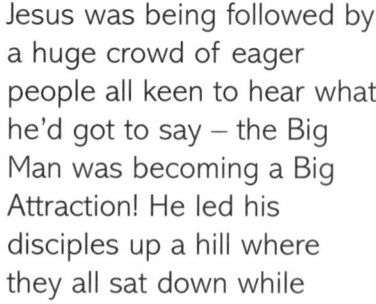

Jesus explained what real happiness was. Some of those listening didn't really understand, because Jesus didn't mention being happy with lots of money, or being happy by having lots of friends. Instead he explained that real happiness is about letting Father God help with the problems of life. He said that sad people, lonely people, weak people and suffering people could all be happy because God would help them get through their hard times.

Then Jesus went on to tell everyone, but his friends in particular: 'Be happy if others hate you and hurt you because you're my friends. God has got a special reward for you.' Jesus' words about happiness were really helpful for many in the crowd, and they still help people now.

What now?
Could you manage without some of the games and toys which make you happy? What about if someone took your computer away? Think about how Jesus describes real happiness.

What else is there?
Read about Jesus talking about happiness: Matthew 5:1-12.

Find out how you should be to be happy: Proverbs 28:20.

16. What's in the family?

Families are strange things! In your family you probably have good times and bad times, happy happenings and dreary days. There are arguments, anger, fun, fights, cuddles and care. You may even look at your friends' family and wish it was yours! Wouldn't it be fun to choose your own family?

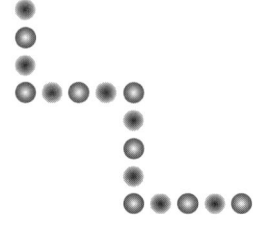

There was a young man who really, really wanted to get away from his family. He had worked on the family farm with his father and brother, but now he was bored – he wanted to see life! 'Dad, give me some money – I want to leave the family and have some fun!' he said. His father was very

sad, but knew it was no use arguing, so he handed his son a great deal of money and off the young man went.

In the big city the young man had a great time. He spent the money on drink and parties, made lots of friends, and became a star. Everyone wanted to know him and spend all his money for him. But soon the money ran out and so did his new pals – they weren't interested in a poor farmer! Starving and lonely, the young man became a farm worker again, this time feeding pigs and even eating the pig food himself. 'I might as well go home and be a farm worker if my dad will have me,' he thought, so he set off back home. His father saw him coming along the farm track and ran out to meet him. His father welcomed him with lots of fuss and put on a celebration meal. 'I thought I had lost my son but now he is back home with the family again!' he said.

What now?
Make a list of the good things and another list of the bad things about your family. Remember that we can't change our family for another one, so we might as well make the best of it!

What else is there?
The full story of the Prodigal Son is worth a look: Luke 15:11-24. Read what the Bible has to say about families: Colossians 3:18-21.

17. What's in worry?

You can always tell when someone worries a lot. Worriers often bite their thumbs or fingers, and fiddle with their hair, jewellery or glasses! They worry about school, they worry about homes and families, they worry about money, and they worry about pop stars. Do you think you are a worrier? If you are, don't worry about it!

Jesus was always trying to get his disciples to stop worrying and trust him – the Big Man! He told them not to worry about feeding the 5,000 people in the crowd; he told them not to worry about the storm in the boat.

As he spoke to his friends and the larger crowd that gathered Jesus knew that many of the people worried a lot.

'Don't worry about food, drink, and clothes,' said Jesus, and he went on to explain that birds don't worry about food, they just get on with being birds and God provides what they need! He told them that God is in control of everything, and we should all concentrate on doing what God wants us to do. 'Don't worry about tomorrow,' said Jesus, and that's what many believe he still says to us.

What now?
Do you worry about things? Who do you tell? Jesus offers to help us all with everything, including our worries.

What else is there?
Read all that Jesus said about worry: Matthew 6:25-34.

Investigate what the writer of Psalm 94 wrote when he was worried: Psalm 94:19.

18. What's in a word?

The word 'open' is used a great deal. We might describe ourselves as being 'open' people with no secrets. We might do tricks and say, 'Open, sesame!'. We may even play at hospitals and do open-heart surgery (but not with real knives, I hope!). Doors open and close, and problems are sometimes described as being 'open-and-shut' cases. I wonder if you are 'open' to learn more about the Big Man – I do hope so!

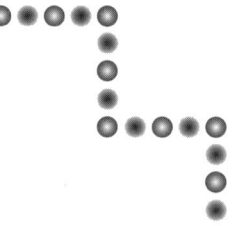

A small group of people was running towards Jesus, helping along another man. Jesus had been busy and was walking with his friends towards the lake, where they hoped for a rest and some quiet. As the small group

got nearer, they called out: 'Jesus, please help our friend. He can't hear and he can't speak.' Jesus was pleased to see them caring for their friend, and stopped to see him. The man looked confused and frightened – he had no idea who Jesus was, what his friends were saying, or why he had been brought to see this strange man.

Jesus knew that the man was worried so he gently led the man away from the crowd, held his head, and said, 'Open!' That moment the man's ears opened up to sound for the first time, and his mouth opened. For the first time he heard himself speak! His friends were thrilled at what happened, but Jesus asked them not to tell people about it. Whether they did or not, word spread – the Big Man could even make deaf and dumb people hear and speak!

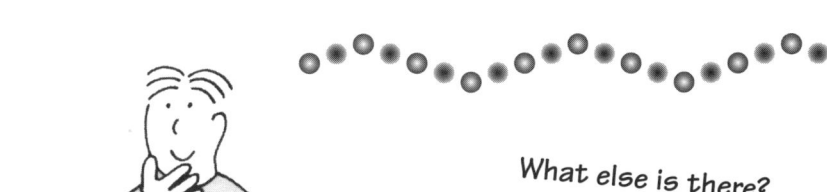

What now?
Open people are people who are willing to listen and find out more. Think about yourself – are you open to learn more about the Big Man?

What else is there?
Read about this healing in full: Mark 7:31-37.

Find out about many of the others Jesus helped: Matthew 15:29-31.

19. What's in foundations?

When you were younger you probably played with basic building blocks. Placed one on top of another they can be used to build towers and houses. But the problem is that they don't have foundations and can easily fall down . . . especially if they are knocked!

Jesus was becoming the Big Man wherever he went and whatever he did. Crowds of people wanted to see him and hear him. He often told people stories to show them how they should live.

One of Jesus' stories was about two house builders.

They each decided to build themselves a house. One chose to build on rock while the other found a nice patch of sand. The man who had chosen the rock to build on used it as a foundation so that when it was built the house was strong enough to withstand the strongest winds and foulest storms. The man who built his house on the sand soon discovered there was a problem. The wet, soft sand didn't make a good foundation, and when the wind and storms came the house fell down.

Jesus told the people listening that they should always build their lives on what God says to do, because otherwise they will fall flat, just like the house on sand.

What now?
We all base our lives on something. How much do you know of God's words and what Jesus said? How much of it do you really understand?

What else is there?
The full story of Jesus' story about house builders: Matthew 7:24-27.

Read more about the wise words of God, and how good it is to obey them: Psalm 119:105-112.

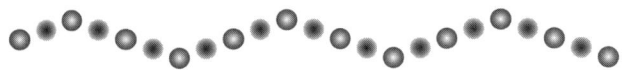

20. What's in a prayer?

There are some things that it is important to learn. When you were young, you learned to say a few words, then you learned your name, and then you went on to learn all the things you know now. But some things are more important to learn than others.

Jesus, the Big Man, and his disciples had escaped from the crowds which followed them around. Jesus went off alone for a while and prayed. The disciples looked puzzled and confused, and even a little bit embarrassed. The prayers

Jesus said were not like the set prayers that they had heard in the synagogues where people worshipped God. Jesus seemed to pray with more life and reality, but they didn't know how!

'Teach us how to pray,' they said to Jesus later. Jesus knew that they wanted to learn how to talk to God, how to thank God for his goodness, how to ask him things and how to say sorry for the things they did wrong. So Jesus taught them some of what we now call *The Lord's Prayer* or *The Family Prayer*. From then on the disciples knew how to talk to God – they had learned one of the most important messages of all!

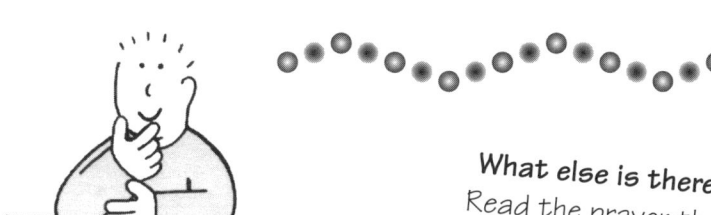

What now?
Do you know The Lord's Prayer? Get hold of a copy and learn it – it's a great prayer, and the Big Man recommends it!

What else is there?
Read the prayer that Jesus taught his friends: Luke 11:1-4.

Read a prayer of thanks to God written hundreds of years before Jesus was born: Psalm 46.

21. What's in a child?

People used to say, 'Children should be seen but not heard!'. I think that's mean and unfair. Children are people just like adults, and have a right to be listened to and given a chance. Do you have a chance to make decisions about things at home or at school?

When Jesus was on the earth most people didn't pay much attention to children. They thought children should be quiet and kept out of the way until they were nearly adults. It was unusual for a man or woman to spend any time with children.

One day Jesus was walking through a small town when some children came running up to him. Immediately Jesus' friends stopped the children. 'Jesus doesn't want to be bothered with you,' they said. But Jesus saw and heard what was happening and gave his disciples a good telling off!
'Let them come to me now,' he said, 'and unless others come to me like these children – happy and willing – they will never know what it is like to be really part of God's plan.'
The disciples, the crowd and even the children looked amazed – no adult had ever treated children with so much love and care before.

What now?
It's not easy being young. There are many things you want to do but you can't! Jesus welcomes all people however young or old they are – do you think Jesus welcomes you?

What else is there?
Have a look at the full story of Jesus and the children: Mark 10:13-16.

See what else the Bible says about children: Psalm 127:3; Colossians 3:21.

22. What's in danger?

Have you ever talked to a flock of sheep? If you have you will know that they are some of the daftest animals around! They wander around following each other, they don't understand what the blaring of a car horn means for them, and they sound so silly with their bleating! But perhaps they talk about us humans being daft, too!

Our Big Man, Jesus, called himself a 'good shepherd', explaining that he had come to help people and lead them the right way through life. Then he told a story about a shepherd and his sheep.

There was a large flock of sheep, perhaps a hundred or more. One night the shepherd was counting them to make sure that they were all safely together, when he realised that one was missing. Meanwhile the one sheep had decided it was bored with the field where they were and had slipped through a gap in the wall. After wandering around and grazing for a while, the sheep realised it was lost and in danger. On its own it could easily be attacked by wild animals, and no one would be there to help.

The shepherd made sure the other sheep were all safe in the sheepfold, and then went searching for the lost one. Finally he found it, bleating sadly a few fields away, lost, cold and scared. 'You were in danger,' said the shepherd, 'but now you are safe again'.

Jesus finished his story by explaining that good shepherds look after all their flock, even the ones that go the wrong way.

What now?
Try to imagine being lost, lonely and in danger like the sheep. Then remember all the people who care about you enough to search for you, find you and keep you safe.

What else is there?
The full story is a good one to read: Luke 15: 1-6.

Read more about Jesus talking on the subject of sheep and shepherds: John 10:1-5.

23. What's in a tree?

Do you know what it's like to be bullied? Have you ever had others call you names? People who are teased and called names often hide away and try to ignore what others say about them, but it still hurts deep down inside.

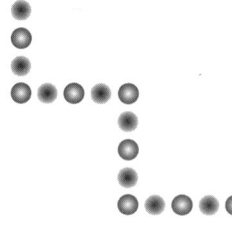

Zacchaeus was bullied. People hated him and called him names. He lived on his own and kept out of the way as much as possible. Zac was unpopular because he was a taxman and a thief! He would call from house to house and collect the taxes for the leaders of the country, but he also took a little extra to keep for himself. He knew he was doing wrong, but it was what all taxmen did.

On the day Jesus was coming to his village, Zac went outside and joined the crowd, but being short, he couldn't see a thing. He jumped up and tried to get a place but people ignored and insulted him. In the end he climbed a tree and watched from there. Before long Jesus came through with his friends, the crowd cheered, and hands reached out to touch him. But Jesus stopped and looked up, straight into the eyes of Zac. The crowd muttered and whispered as Jesus said, 'Come down – I want to have tea with you'. Zac was amazed, delighted and scared all at once. At last someone cared about him . . . but Jesus seemed to know about Zac's cheating. After they had talked, Zac changed into a really cool person; he gave back the money he had taken wrongly, and he found that people didn't hate him anymore.

What now?
Have you ever bullied or teased someone? Was it fair to be unkind? Have a think about how the other people treated Zac and compare how Jesus treated Zac.

What else is there?
Read the full Zac story, from being hated to giving money away: Luke 19:2-8.

Have a look at the story of another man who wanted to change, but didn't want to give up his money: Luke 18:18-23.

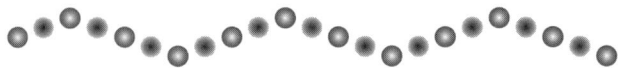

24. What's in a crowd?

It's really great to be near someone famous and important. Have you ever stood in a crowd on the roadside, cheering for a famous person to go by, in the hope that you might just catch a quick glimpse of them? It's dead exciting!

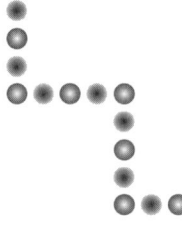

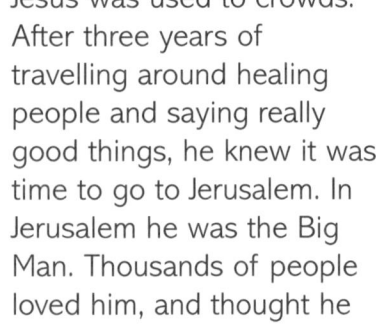

Jesus was used to crowds. After three years of travelling around healing people and saying really good things, he knew it was time to go to Jerusalem. In Jerusalem he was the Big Man. Thousands of people loved him, and thought he

was their hero. They hoped he would become a king and get an army to fight the Romans. Only the Romans, who ruled the country, and the religious leaders, who liked their own power, thought Jesus was a troublemaker.

For the last part of his journey to the big city Jesus was given a small donkey to ride on. When the crowds saw him in the distance they cheered and shouted. Some pulled long leaves from the palm trees around them and waved them, others took off their coats and cloaks, laying them on the road for Jesus' donkey to walk over. As they listened to the cheering and shouting, his friends finally realised just how special Jesus was – he really was the Son of God!

What now?
If Jesus were to be walking down your road in a few minutes, would you go out and cheer for him? Do you think the Big Man is worth it?

What else is there?
Read about the amazing arrival at Jerusalem: Luke 19:28-40.

Have a look at the warning Jesus gave his disciples, which they didn't understand: Luke 18:31-34.

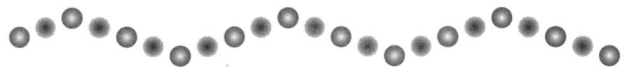

25. What's in a meal?

Do you like food? Most of us really enjoy food, and have favourite meals. Maybe you really like fish and chips, or perhaps pizza is your favourite. Maybe you are really into sweet things, and eat ice cream by the bucketful!

It was Passover, a special time, like a holiday, and most people had a special get-together at that time of year. Jesus and his disciples were having a meal together. Jesus knew that in the next few days he would be arrested and killed, but even though he had warned his friends, they didn't really understand.

'Look this way,' said Jesus, as they sat around a large mat on the floor and ate together. Then Jesus picked up the bread and broke it. 'This is like my body,' he said. 'It will be broken for you and for all people.' Then, while the disciples were trying to understand what he meant, he picked up the wine. 'This is like my blood,' he said. 'It will be poured out for you and all people. Remember me when I've gone by sharing bread and wine together.'

Only later did the Big Man's friends really understand what he had done at that meal, which we now call The Last Supper.

What now?
We all celebrate things with meals. Make a list of the special meals you and your family have, which might include Easter, Christmas, birthdays, as well as other times. In most churches people remember Jesus by taking bread and wine together like Jesus and his friends did.

What else is there?
Look at the story of Jesus and his disciples having that meal together: Matthew 26:26-30.

Read the same story again, told by Paul, one of Jesus' followers: 1 Corinthians 11:23-25.

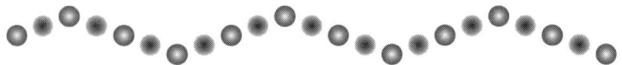

26. What's in the garden?

Most people like to get away and have some time to themselves. Some dads disappear off into the garden shed, and many children like to hide away in their bedrooms to escape brothers and sisters! Do you have a favourite place to sneak away to?

The Big Man was nearing the biggest test of all – he was going to die! He knew that he was going to suffer as he led the disciples into a large garden on the edge of Jerusalem. 'I am going to pray,' he told them. 'Wait here until I come back'.

Jesus found a quiet corner of the garden and cried out to Father God, telling him how much he feared having to suffer and die. But he knew he had to do it, so he asked God for the strength to go through with it all. When he got back to his friends they had fallen asleep, so he woke them just in time to see a group of soldiers coming towards them. 'Are you going to arrest me now?' Jesus asked them. 'You could have arrested me in the temple instead – that's where I have been speaking every day.' Once they were sure it was Jesus the soldiers arrested him and took him away to the court house, where he was mocked and spat on and beaten.

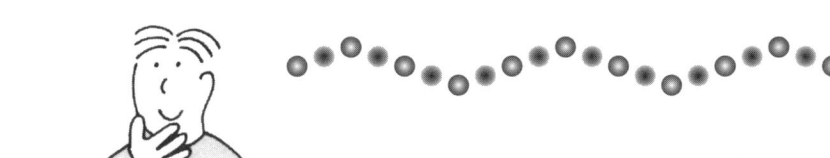

What now?
Think about Jesus. He didn't want to die, but he knew that he had to. What do you do that you don't really feel like doing? Jesus got help from Father God when he needed the strength to keep going.

What else is there?
Look at the full story, and find out who got injured: Luke 22:47-53.

Find out what happened when Jesus was questioned by the religious leaders: Mark 14:53-65.

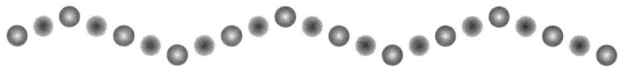

27. What's in a death?

> Death is a sad subject. Most of us don't really want to die, and we've known the sadness when a pet, a friend or a relative has died. But death can lead to good things too, like this death.

The crowds of people had realised that Jesus wasn't going to lead an army against the Romans, so they had turned against him. The religious leaders didn't want to lose their power, so they had turned against him. By lying and cheating they managed to have him sentenced to die like criminals did at that time – they planned to hang him on a large cross made from two pieces of rough wood.

As the cross was prepared and Jesus was nailed onto it through his wrists and ankles, his mother cried, and his friends looked shocked and stunned. Only a few days before Jesus had been a hero, now he was dying as a thief. People spat at him and made fun of him, others made a crown out of long, sharp thorns and pushed it onto his head. They stole all he had, and stood watching him on the cross. The sky went very dark and Jesus cried out in pain to his Father God, before his head sank down – he was dead. That could have been the end of the story, but the Big Man's story goes on right up until today!

What now?
Think about the pain and suffering Jesus went through. He said he did it to take on himself all the wrong things everyone does, and to stop us feeling guilty. If it's true, do you think that's an amazing thing to do?

What else is there?
Read one of these reports of the death of Jesus:
Mark 15:21-41;
Luke 23:26-49.

28. What's in the tomb?

Every day the news on TV seems to be bad, and it's easy to start believing that everything in the world is bad. But bad news is always followed by good news sooner or later . . . although sometimes the wait can be long and boring!

Jesus, the Big Man, had died. To make sure he wasn't pretending, the soldiers waiting near the cross stabbed him in the side. Then they let some of his friends take him away to a small cave that was to be his tomb. There his body

was wrapped in strips of cloth and he was left, a large stone being rolled in front of the entrance to seal the tomb.

Jesus' family and friends were all very upset. They had heard Jesus say that he would come alive again, but they didn't really understand it. On the third day after he had died some women went to check the tomb and were shocked to find it wide open, the stone having been moved. Inside there was no body, but instead two men appeared, looking like angels in shining clothes. 'Why are you looking here for a body?' the angels asked. 'Don't you remember that Jesus promised to come alive again?' The women were speechless, and ran back to tell the disciples as quickly as they could. Jesus was alive, and is alive today!

What now?
How could that stone move from the tomb? How could a dead man come alive again? It is either just a made-up story that millions of silly people have been fool enough to believe, or it is true. What do you think?

What else is there?
That story of the empty tomb is well worth a look: Luke 24:1-10.

There's another good story about the tomb too: Matthew 28:1-10.

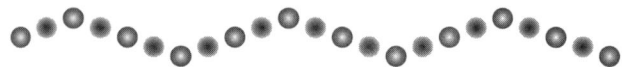

29. What's in a touch?

Have you ever had the chance to touch something really precious or very old? You may have touched an ancient fossil (no, I don't mean your granny!) or a precious piece of jewellery. Somehow, touching something makes us more sure that it's real.

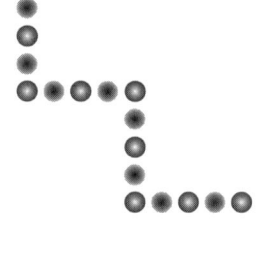

Eyes popped out of heads when Jesus was seen walking and talking just three days after he had died! The same people who had seen the sky go dark and watched Jesus gasp his last breath now claimed to have spoken to him. It was like being in the middle of a dream for Thomas, one of Jesus' best mates. But a nagging voice inside his head told him it would all come to an end and he'd wake up.

Jesus walked into their room one morning, and while the other followers were delighted, Thomas knew that his eyes alone would never be able to prove that his leader really was real. He wanted to go one step further – he wanted to touch. Jesus told him to put his finger on the wounds in his hands and side, and Thomas knew then that Jesus was really alive.

Since then millions have also believed, without having seen Jesus hang on the cross, and without needing to see or touch him.

What now?
None of us can see the wind – we only see its results. Think about all the things you believe in that you can't see.

What else is there?
Read about Jesus meeting with his mates: John 20:24-29.
Read about another time Jesus met with them: Luke 24:36-44.

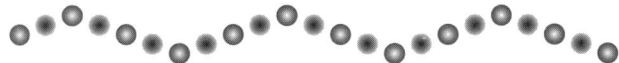

30. What's in your heart?

There are many other stories about Jesus in the Bible. Some are so amazing that it's really hard to believe that they could have happened, yet the Bible says that God can do anything. It's one thing to know a few facts and stories in your head, but it's quite another to believe them in your heart.

2,000 years have passed since the Big Man, Jesus, lived on earth. Yet in those years many people have trusted in him, learned the stories in their heads, and found that they believed it all in their hearts too. Churches have been built, millions of people across the world gather like the disciples did to remember and worship Jesus. And the story goes on as every day more people get to know Jesus better.

You can ask any Christians you know more about Jesus, the biggest man ever, the Big Man who changed history. You can write to me at the address in the front of this book, or just find some time to sit quietly and read more from the Bible about him.

What now?
Now you know more about Jesus, the Big Man who lived 2,000 years ago. Do you think it's just a good story, or is there more to it than that? Think about it!

What else is there?
Read what Jesus said about himself:
John 3:16;
John 6:35;
John 8:12.